NOTE

Dating as far back as the 7th century B.C., the twelve symbols of the Zodiac have often been incorporated into art. In ancient times they appeared in architecture or illustrated prayer books, and more recently, artists have featured the Zodiac in paintings, sculpture, fashion, and the popular medium of stained glass. An especially appealing complement to the Zodiac, stained glass lends a mystical quality to the ancient symbols.

The images in this book are specially designed patterns for stained glass. Use your imagination to create lampshades, ornaments, windows, or any other craft project. Although the patterns in this book are immediately useful, they may also be reproduced in larger or smaller sizes.

This collection of patterns is intended as a supplement to stained glass instruction books (such as *Stained Glass Craft Made Simple* by James McDonell, Dover Publications, Inc., 0-486-24963-8). All materials needed, included general instructions and tools for beginners, can usually be purchased from local craft and hobby stores, or on the Internet.

Zodiac
Stained Glass
Pattern Book

ANNA CROYLE

DOVER PUBLICATIONS, INC.
Mineola, New York

Planet Friendly Publishing
✔ Made in the United States
✔ Printed on Recycled Paper
Text: 30%   Cover: 10%
Learn more: www.greenedition.org

GREEN
EDITION

At Dover Publications we're committed to producing books in an earth-friendly manner and to helping our customers make greener choices.

Manufacturing books in the United States ensures compliance with strict environmental laws and eliminates the need for international freight shipping, a major contributor to global air pollution.

And printing on recycled paper helps minimize our consumption of trees, water and fossil fuels. The text of *Zodiac Stained Glass Pattern Book* was printed on paper made with 30% post-consumer waste, and the cover was printed on paper made with 10% post-consumer waste. According to Environmental Defense's Paper Calculator, by using this innovative paper instead of conventional papers, we achieved the following environmental benefits:

**Trees Saved: 11 • Air Emissions Eliminated: 1,034 pounds
Water Saved: 4,983 gallons • Solid Waste Eliminated: 303 pounds**

For more information on our environmental practices, please visit us online at www.doverpublications.com/green

Copyright

Bibliographical Note

Zodiac Stained Glass Pattern Book is a new work, first published by Dover Publications, Inc., in 2010.

International Standard Book Number
ISBN-13: 978-0-486-47499-1
ISBN-10: 0-486-47499-2

Manufactured in the United States by Courier Corporation
47499201
www.doverpublications.com

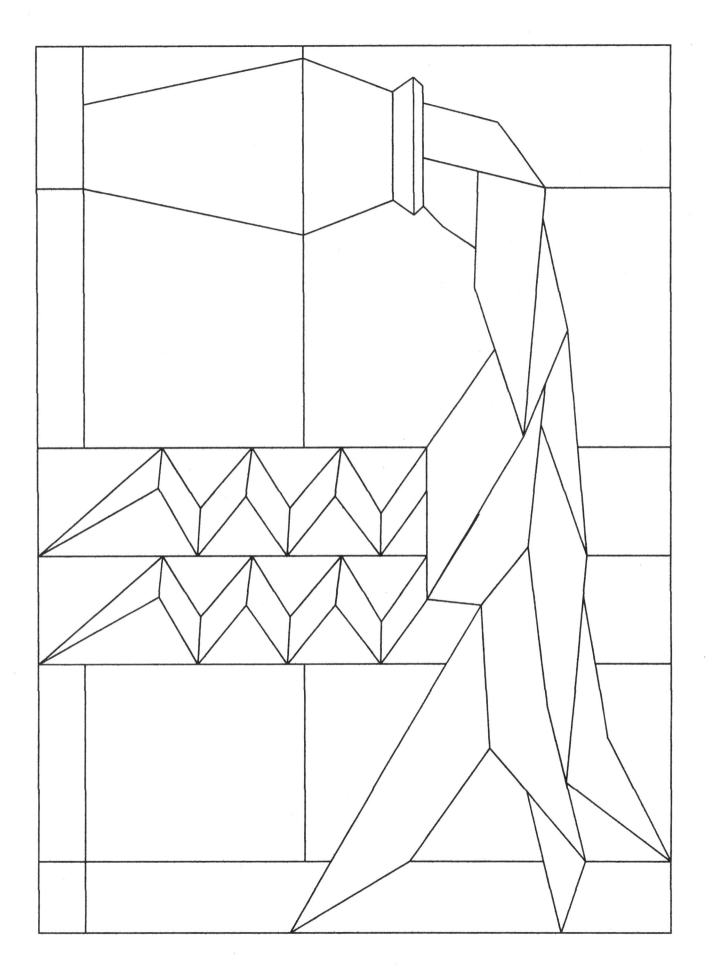

Aquarius (January 20–February 18)   1

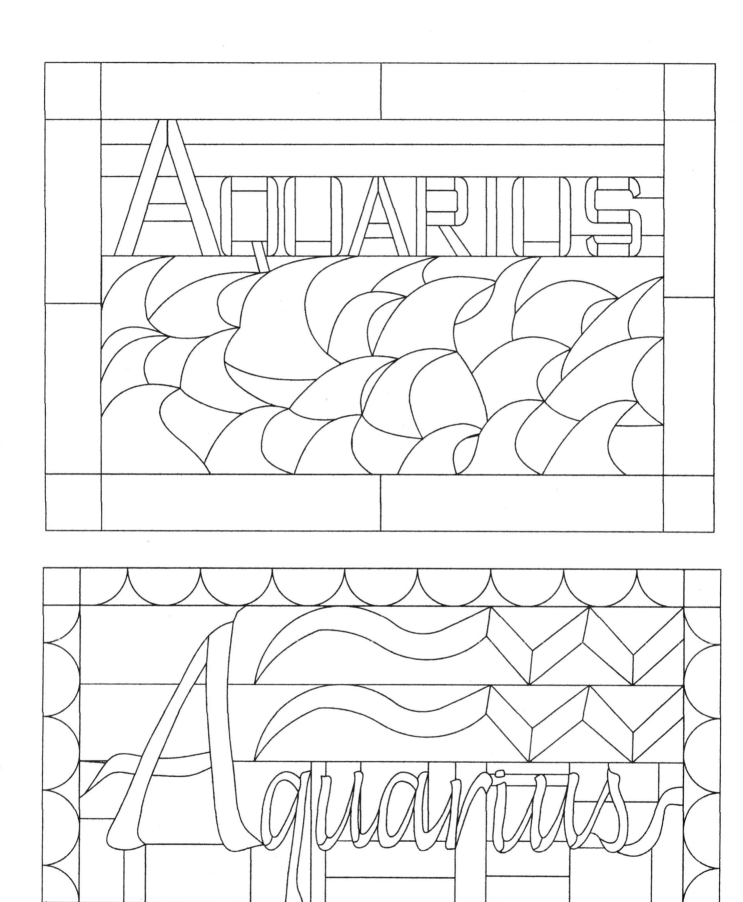

2 *Aquarius* (January 20–February 18)

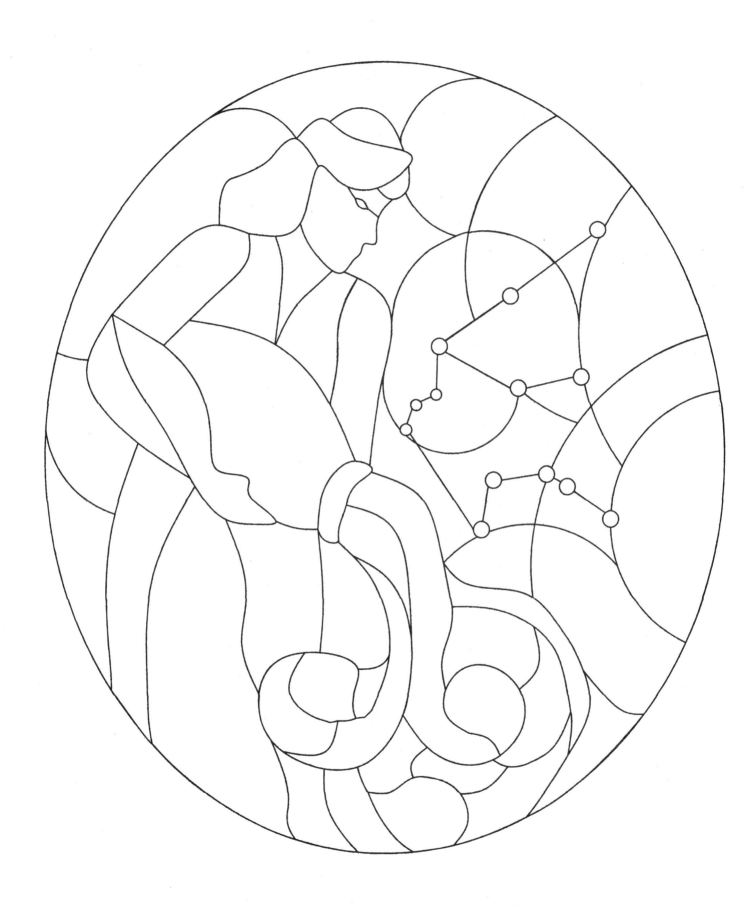

4   *Aquarius* (January 20–February 18)

Pisces (February 19–March 20)   5

6 *Pisces* (February 19–March 20)

Pisces (February 19–March 20)   7

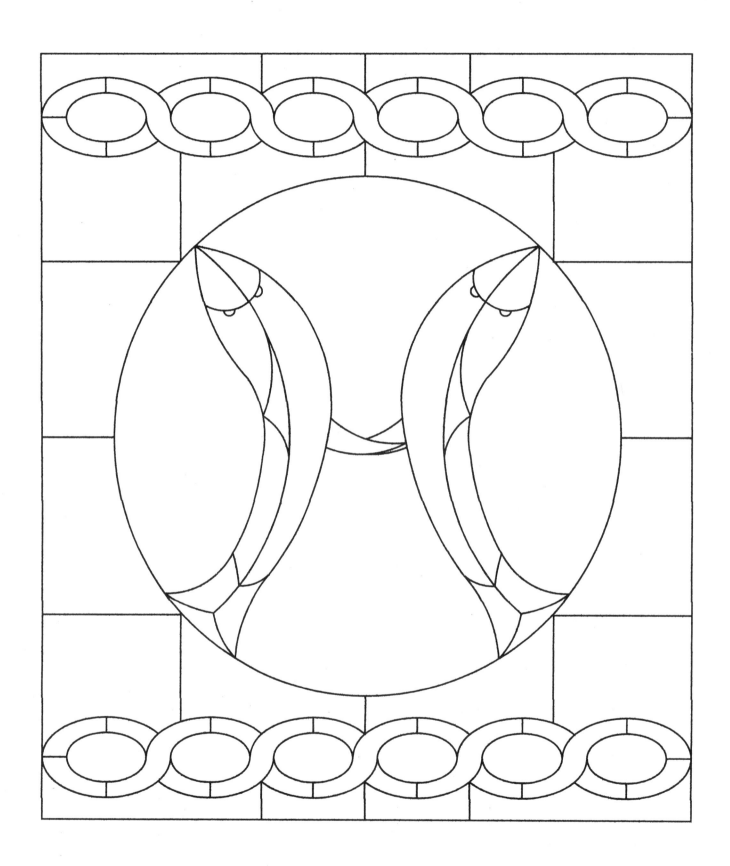

8 *Pisces* (February 19–March 20)

10 *Aries* (March 21–April 19)

12   *Aries* (March 21–April 19)

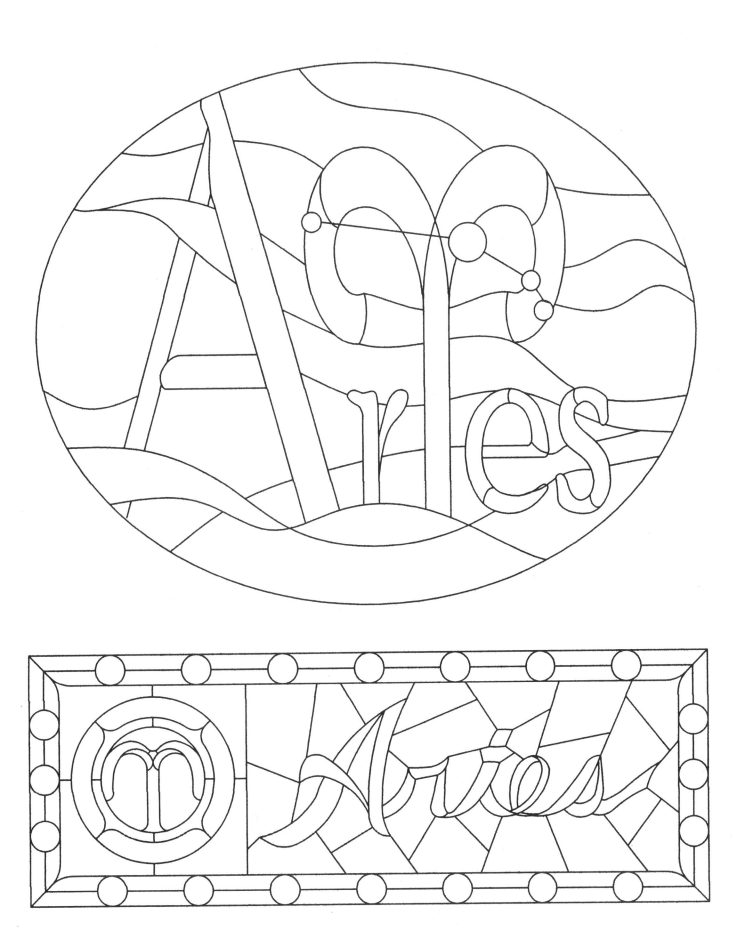

Aries (March 21–April 19)   13

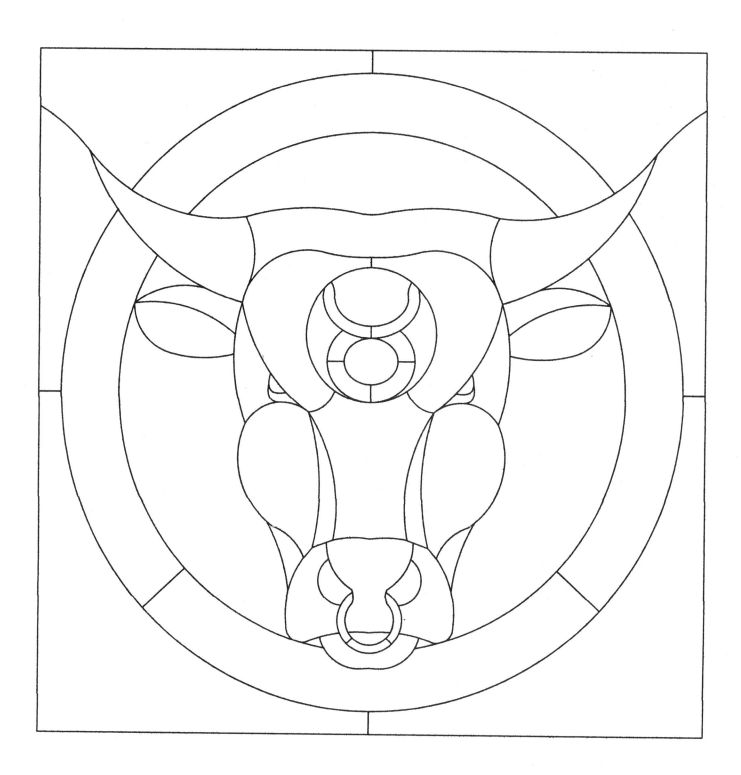

14   *Taurus* (April 20–May 20)

16   *Taurus* (April 20–May 20)

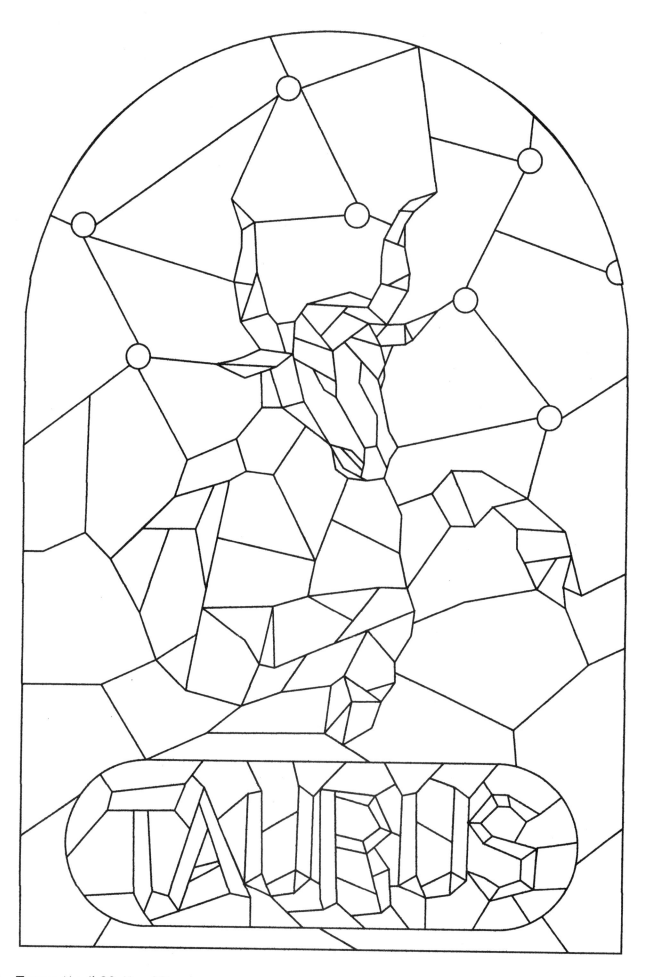

18   *Taurus* (April 20–May 20)

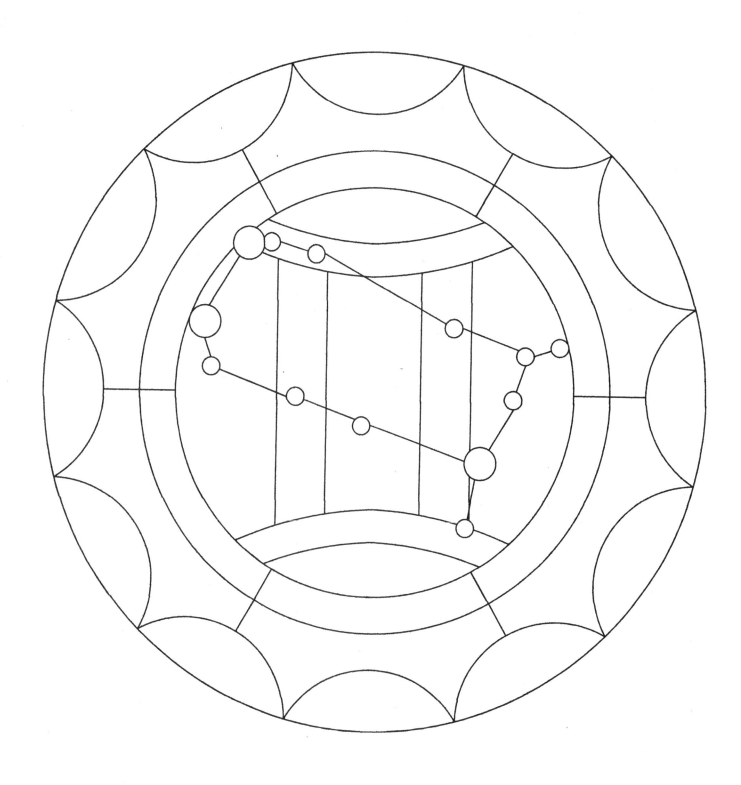

20   *Gemini* (May 21–June 21)

22   *Gemini* (May 21–June 21)

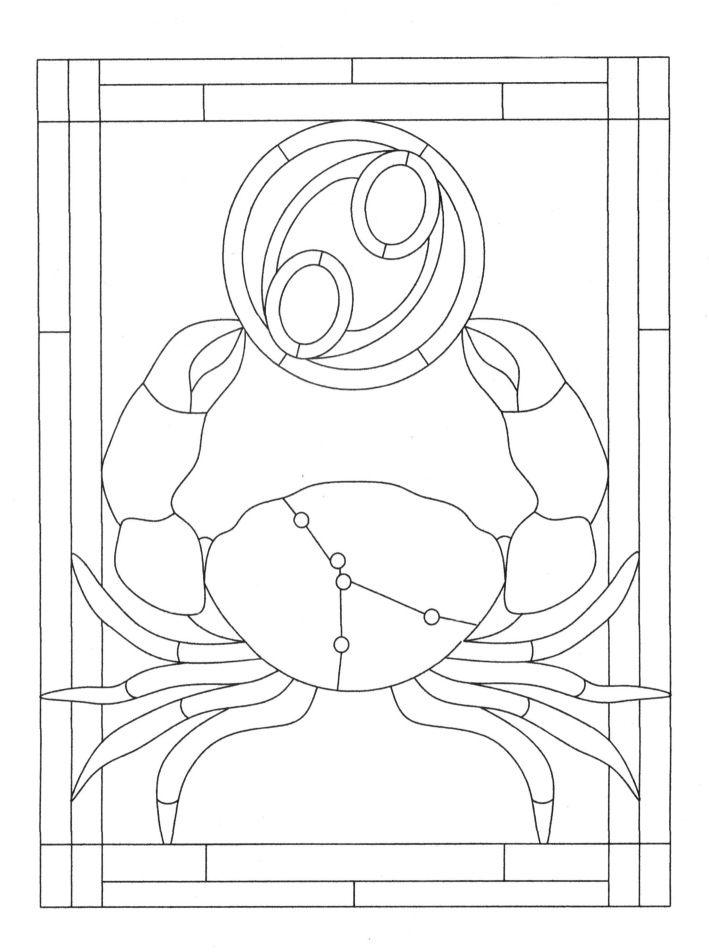

24   *Cancer* (June 22–July 22)

Cancer (June 22–July 22)   25

Cancer (June 22–July 22)

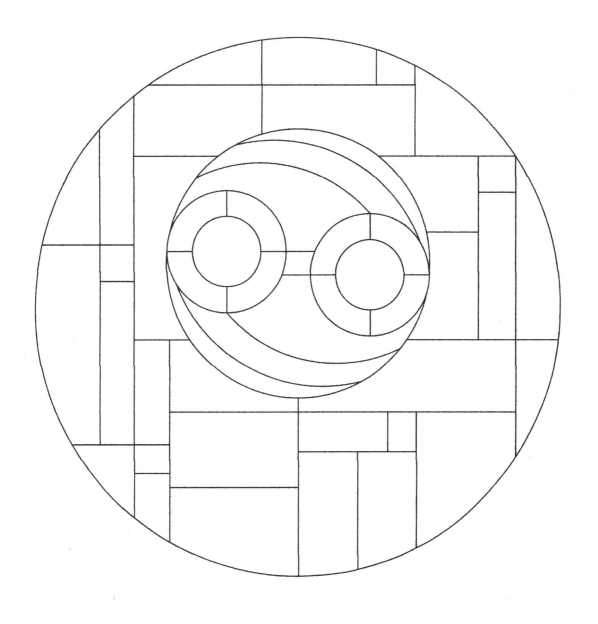

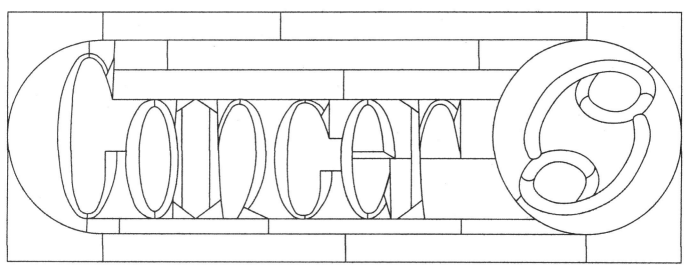

28   *Leo* (July 23–August 22)

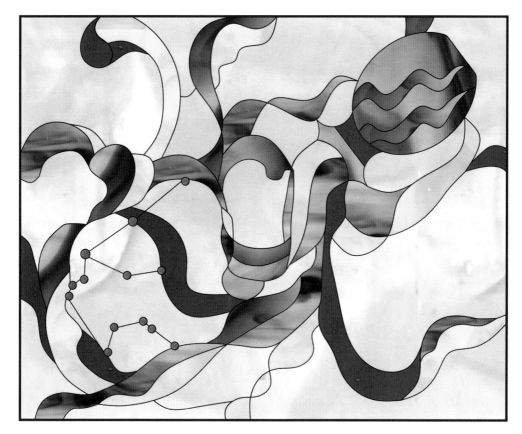

Page 3

Page 2

Page 6

Page 5

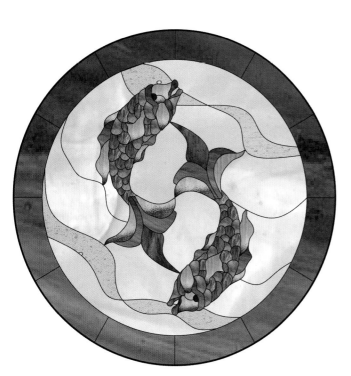

Page 7

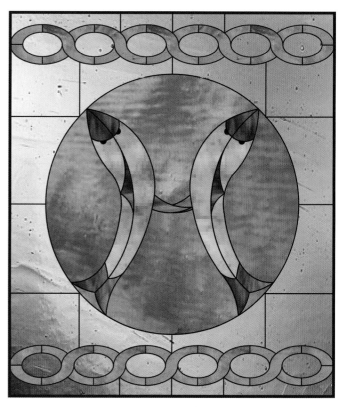

Page 8

Page 9

Page 10

Page 12

Page 11

Page 13

Page 13

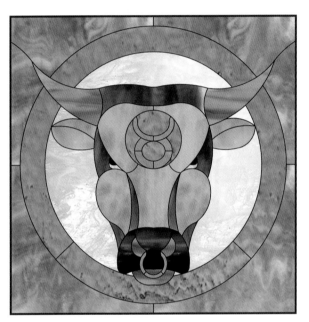

Page 14

Page 15

Page 16

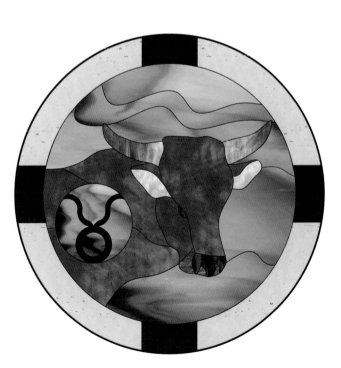

Page 17

Page 18

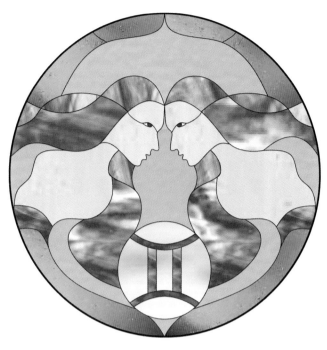

Page 19

Page 20

Page 22

Page 21

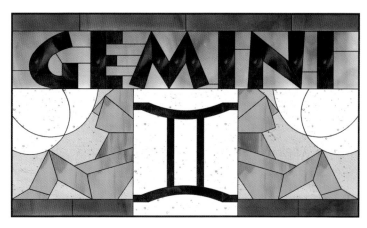

Page 23

Page 24

Page 25

Page 27

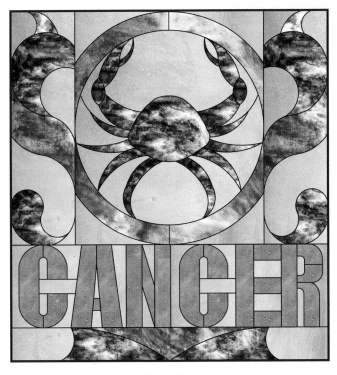

Page 26

Page 27

Page 28

Page 29

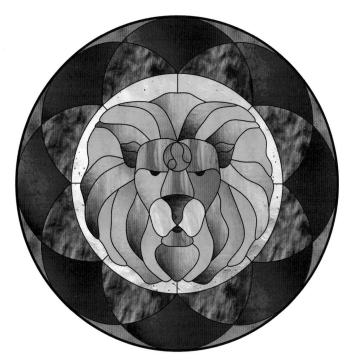

Page 30

Page 31

Page 31

Page 32

Page 33

Page 35

Page 36

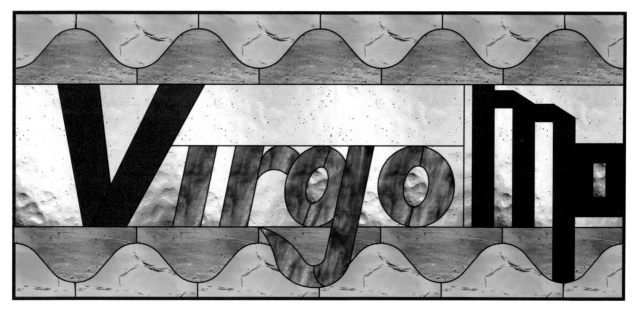

Page 34

Page 37

Page 39

Page 40

Page 40

Page 41

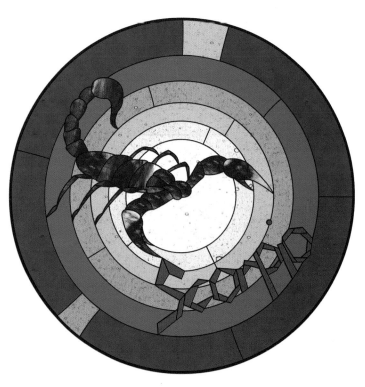

Page 42

Page 43

Page 44

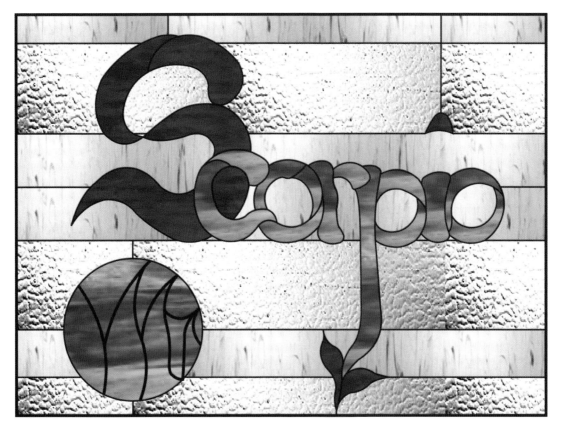

Page 45

Page 47

Page 46

Page 48

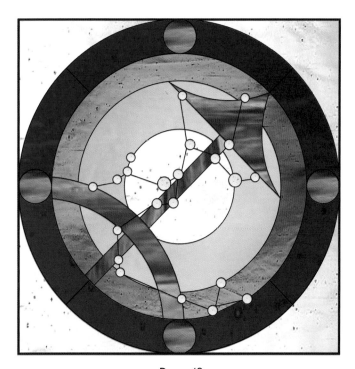

Page 49

Page 50

Page 51

Page 52

Page 53

Page 54

Page 55

Page 56

Page 57

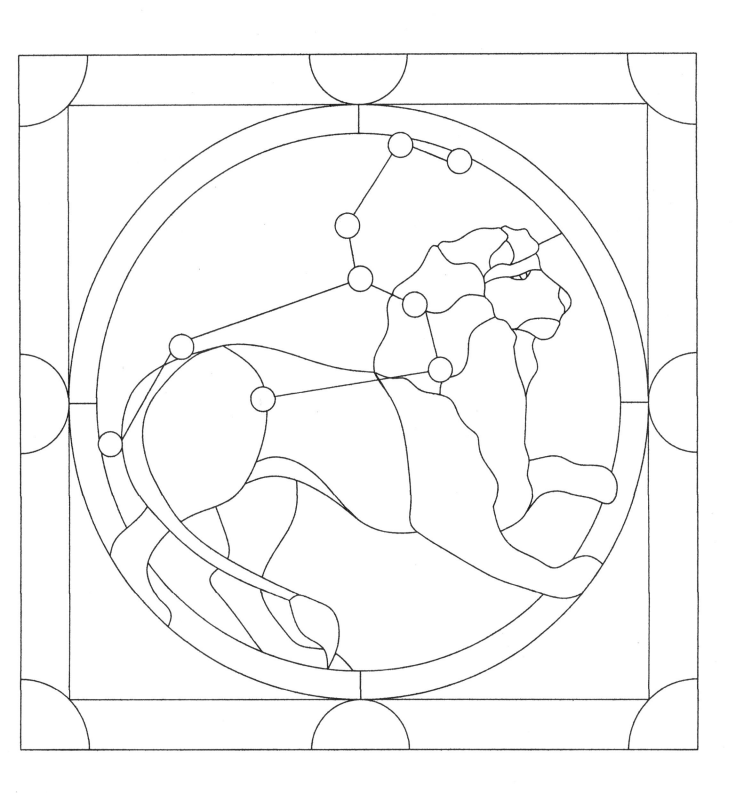

Leo (July 23–August 22) 29

Leo (July 23–August 22)

32 *Virgo* (August 23–September 22)

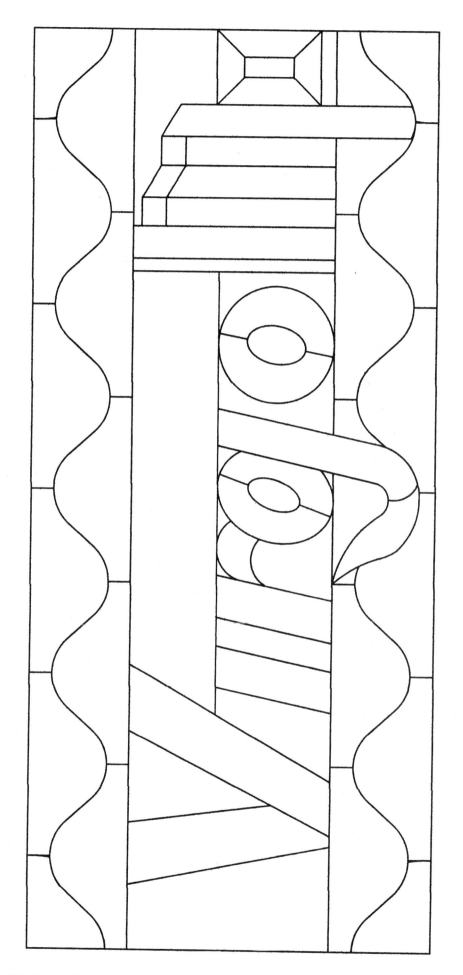

34   *Virgo* (August 23–September 22)

36   *Virgo* (August 23–September 22)

Libra (September 23–October 23)   37

38　*Libra* (September 23–October 23)

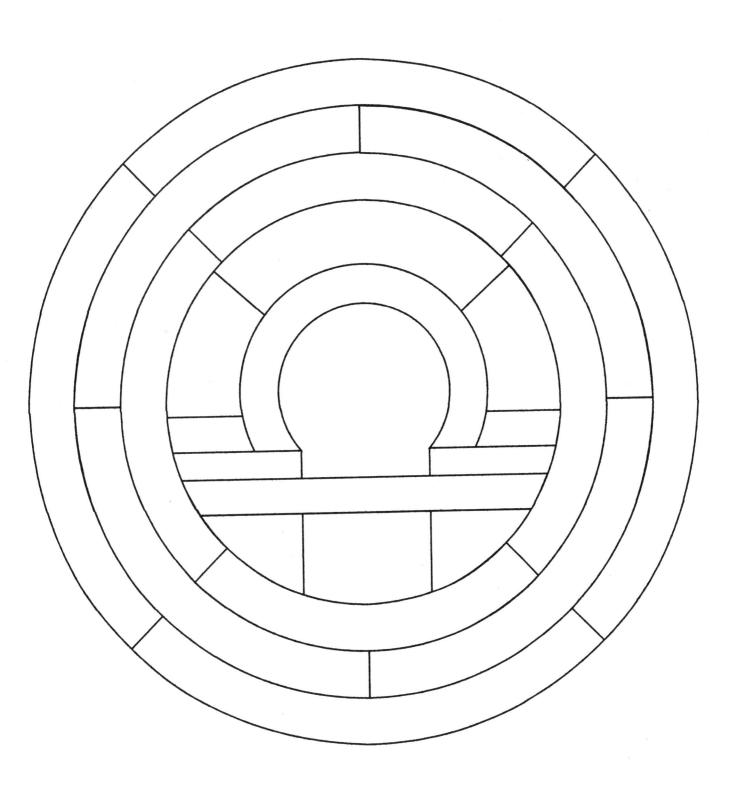

40 *Libra* (September 23–October 23)

42   *Scorpio* (October 24–November 21)

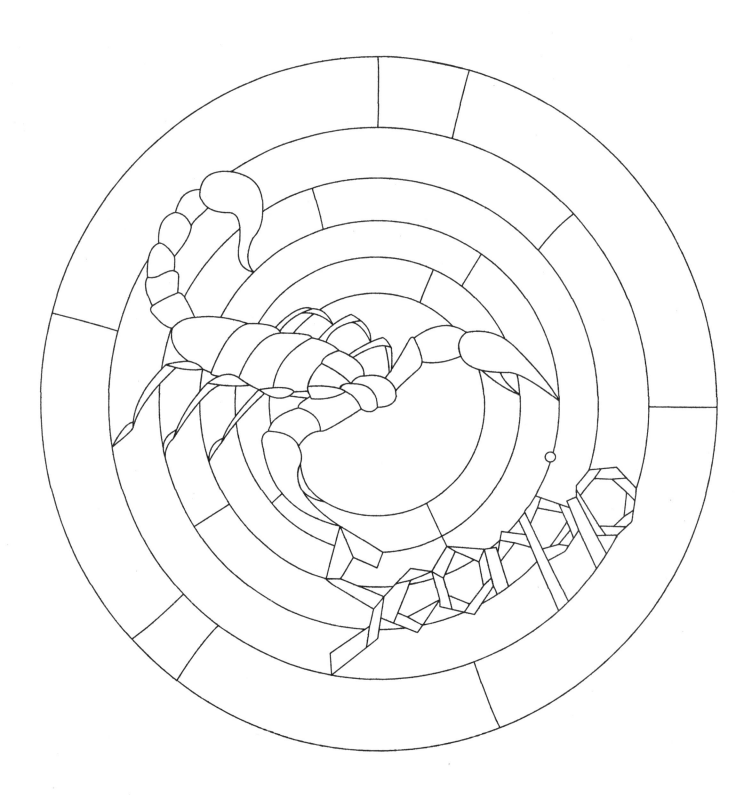

44   *Scorpio* (October 24–November 21)

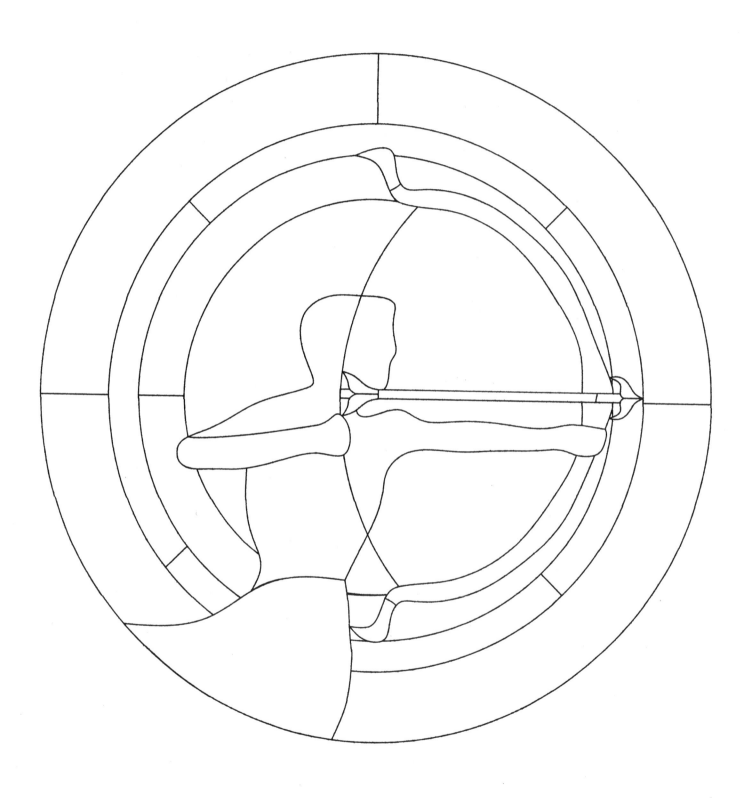

46 *Sagittarius* (November 22–December 21)

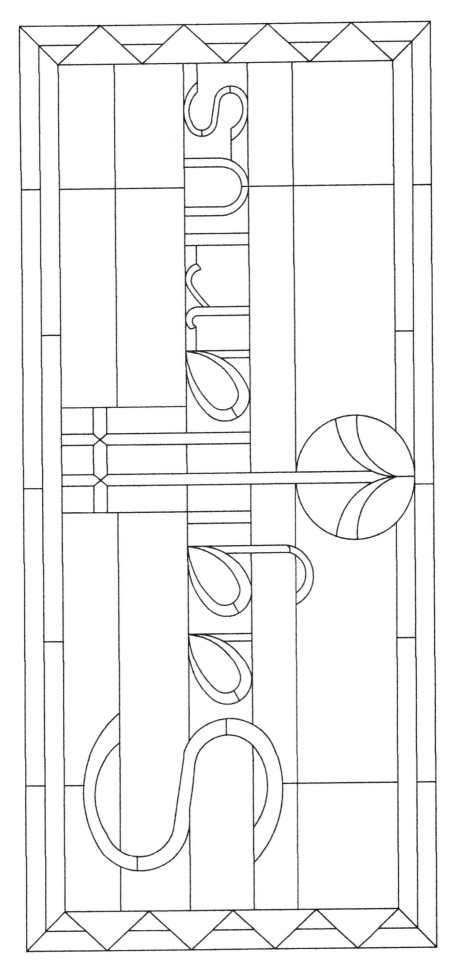

Sagittarius (November 22–December 21) 47

48 *Sagittarius* (November 22–December 21)

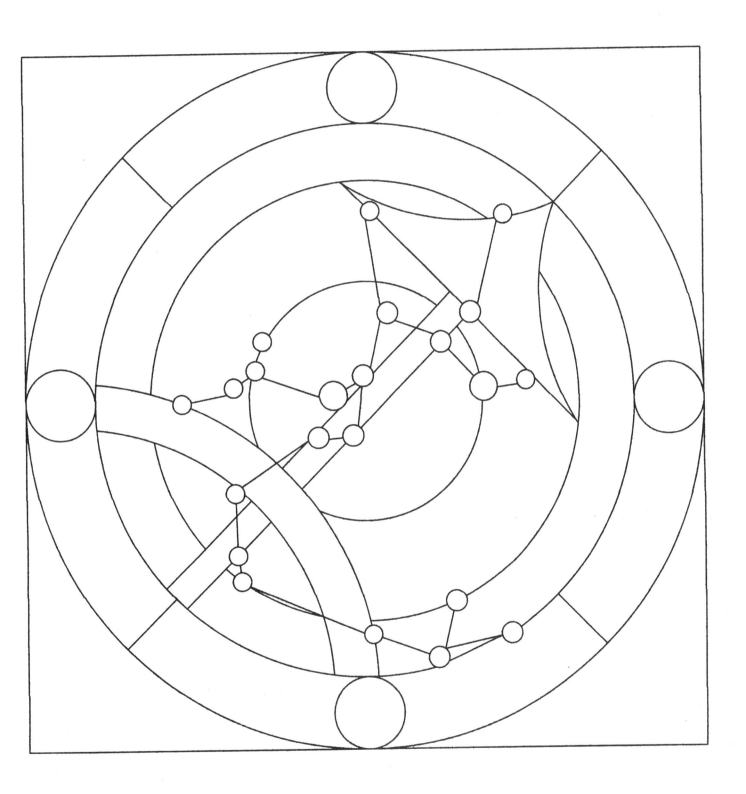

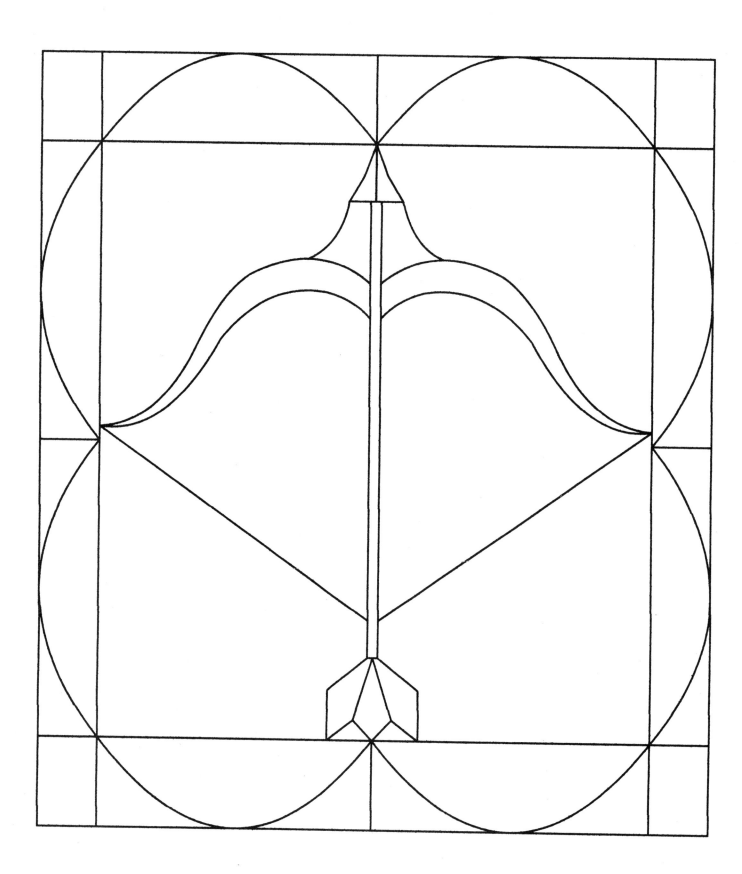

Sagittarius (November 22–December 21)

52 *Capricorn* (December 22–January 19)

54   *Capricorn* (December 22–January 19)

Capricorn (December 22–January 19) 55